MAY   2017

SandCastle

Rhyme Time

The Waste IS Traced

Anders Hanson

Consulting Editor, Diane Craig, M.A./Reading Specialist

ABDO
Publishing Company

Published by ABDO Publishing Company, 4940 Viking Drive, Edina, Minnesota 55435.

Printed in the United States.

Credits
Edited by: Pam Price
Curriculum Coordinator: Nancy Tuminelly
Cover and Interior Design and Production: Mighty Media
Photo Credits: BananaStock Ltd., Brand X Pictures, Comstock, Corel, Creatas, Eyewire Images, Hemera, PhotoDisc, Stockbyte

Library of Congress Cataloging-in-Publication Data

Hanson, Anders, 1980-
    The waste is traced / Anders Hanson.
        p. cm. -- (Rhyme time)
    Includes index.
    ISBN 1-59197-820-3 (hardcover)
    ISBN 1-59197-926-9 (paperback)
    1. English language--Rhyme--Juvenile literature. I. Title. II. Rhyme time (ABDO Publishing Company)

PE1517.H379 2004
428.1'3--dc22

2004049110

SandCastle™ books are created by a professional team of educators, reading specialists, and content developers around five essential components that include phonemic awareness, phonics, vocabulary, text comprehension, and fluency. All books are written, reviewed, and leveled for guided reading, early intervention reading, and Accelerated Reader® programs and designed for use in shared, guided, and independent reading and writing activities to support a balanced approach to literacy instruction.

Let Us Know

After reading the book, SandCastle would like you to tell us your stories about reading. What is your favorite page? Was there something hard that you needed help with? Share the ups and downs of learning to read. We want to hear from you! To get posted on the ABDO Publishing Company Web site, send us e-mail at:

sandcastle@abdopub.com

SandCastle Level: Fluent

Words that rhyme do not have to be spelled the same. These words rhyme with each other:

based

raced

faced

taste

haste

traced

waist

misplaced

waste

paste

George is reading a book that is based on a true story.

Ivy is late for school.

She will miss the math quiz if she doesn't make **haste**.

5

Victor **faced** the class and read his essay.

Nate cuts out shapes that he will stick together with **paste**.

Melissa found her teddy bear.
When her family moved, it had
been **misplaced**.

Abigail likes the way strawberries taste.

Lynn and her friends raced across the beach.

Vanessa spins four hoops around her **waist**.

Kathy's mom traced Kathy's hand.

Mr. Butler's class is spending the day at the beach picking up **waste**.

The Waste IS Traced

There once was a sculpture made of waste.

Some people liked it, others said it lacked taste.

But suddenly it was stolen,
or perhaps misplaced.

The case was based
on a woman who faced
a man who raced
from the scene with haste.

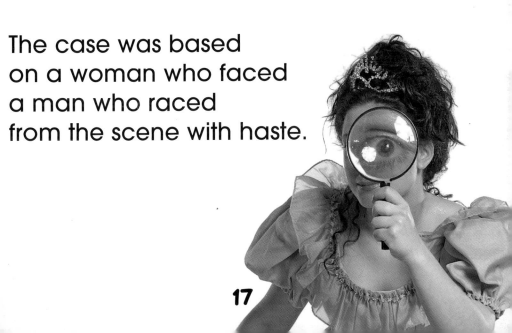

Clues were found
and eventually were traced

back to the house where
the waste had been placed.

Away from the house,
the masked man raced.

He knew that he was being chased.

He was finally grabbed
around the waist.

The sculpture was replaced

and a stiff penalty faced.

What do you call
glue that is not where it belongs?

Misplaced paste

Glossary

essay. a short paper about a single subject

haste. rapidly; the phrase *make haste* means hurry

misplace. to lose something or put it in the wrong place

sculpture. a three-dimensional work of art

waste. garbage

About SandCastle™

A professional team of educators, reading specialists, and content developers created the SandCastle™ series to support young readers as they develop reading skills and strategies and increase their general knowledge. The SandCastle™ series has four levels that correspond to early literacy development in young children. The levels are provided to help teachers and parents select the appropriate books for young readers.

Emerging Readers
(no flags)

Beginning Readers
(1 flag)

Transitional Readers
(2 flags)

Fluent Readers
(3 flags)

These levels are meant only as a guide. All levels are subject to change.

To see a complete list of SandCastle™ books and other nonfiction titles from ABDO Publishing Company, visit www.abdopub.com or contact us at:
4940 Viking Drive, Edina, Minnesota 55435 • 1-800-800-1312 • fax: 1-952-831-1632